10526

822

L

C000233713

Sch
This book is due for return on
ᴊᴇʟᴏᴡ.

New York-Toronto-Hollywood

RAINBOW'S ENDING

The play was first performed by the Tricycle Youth Theatre in
November 1984 with the following cast:

Siobhan Callaghan
Karen Clancy
Siavaun Clarke
Robert Ewen
Marc Holland
Jenny Jules
Neema Kambona
Kate Lawton
Patrick Montague
Fiona O'Donnell
Neran Persaud
Chris Pitsalis
Sonia Stewart
Steve Swainbank

Directed by Paddi Taylor
Produced by Maureen Simpson

COPYRIGHT INFORMATION
(See also page ii)

AUTHOR'S NOTES

The Making of the Play

I was asked to write a play for a large, mix-race group of young people in London, working from the Tricycle Theatre in Kilburn. We met on a weekly basis over a month or so and, under the leadership of director Paddi Taylor, explored various themes and ideas. Towards the end of that process the themes of group loyalty, power and individual choice began to emerge. My task then was to find a storyline within which to develop those ideas. It was a wonderful, inventive and imaginative group, well aware of the problems facing anyone growing up in a tough urban environment, but certainly not daunted by life. Instinctively I decided I was not going to give them yet another "depressed youth growing up in inner-city blight" type of play. I wanted something that would reflect their own vigour and sheer joy of life, whilst also engaging with big, important issues. A modern "fable" seemed appropriate, as did a storytelling style, which would give free rein to imaginative performing, unencumbered with the conventional trappings of theatre. After the first few worries about the style ("Yes it's a good story but how do you turn it into a play?") there were no problems. Indeed, whereas many trained actors are taught that to "act" is to be someone else entirely, these young people I worked with had much less trouble beginning from the basis of: "Here I am on this stage, this is me and I'm going to tell you a story, and it goes like this ..."

A Note on Storytelling Theatre

In this style of theatre the performer acts as both character and narrator. This is not a conventional script, with stage directions, lists of props used, scenic instructions and character descriptions. Instead, all this information is contained within what the performer is given to speak. In its simplest form, a play like *Rainbow's Ending* could be performed by one (very skilful) actor with nothing but her or his body and voice to create all the characters and bring to life all of the narrative. Conversely, it may be presented by a large group of people and with even the addition of more traditional theatre effects (lighting changes, music, etc).

This may at first seem daunting: how to bring alive a play in which the traditional "signposts" and conventional effects that we associate with "theatre" are absent. In fact, storytelling theatre is the oldest form of theatre: think of the person on their mat in the African market surrounded by an audience, retelling an old and complicated myth with only the aid of perhaps a piece of cloth or a musical instrument. Indeed, we all "storytell", when we re-enact incidents that have happened to us — sketching in the scene, the action, with snatches of dialogue and commentary. I have often found that an excellent way into this style is to start with simple exercises based on the telling of incidents that have happened to us during the day. We find out the ways we all naturally have of bringing to life things that have taken place: think of someone excitedly repeating and showing what happened in a playground fight, or in the cinema queue, or at the football match, or in assembly yesterday.

The key to the style is essentially that everything is *animated* — by this I mean that the lines which are narrative are worked on to have as much life, vigour and physical action attached to them as the "dialogue" lines. There is no "neutral" in this style of theatre.

To give one small example. In SCENE 1 performer G has the line: "I'm bigger than you," one of them boasted.

Now, the narrative part of the line ('one of them boasted') gives the key as to how the dialogue part of the line ("'I'm bigger than you'") could be delivered — that is "boastfully". But this does not mean that once the performer has delivered the dialogue, he or she then slips into a flat monotone for the narrative. Indeed, here is the fun of this style, for the task is then to discover how best to deliver "one of them boasted'. There could be a number of choices:

1. To carry on in the manner of the word, as it were, and deliver the line "boastfully" (ie to deliver it "in character').

2. To step outside the character and comment *on* the character to the audience in a sort of aside: "one of them boasted" could then be delivered with a whole other meaning — that is, "isn't this giant a bore, going around boasting all the time?"

3. To deliver the line totally "unboastfully" (fearfully, perhaps), so giving an indication of the character's *real* feelings (ie "I'm only boasting because I'm really timid').

This is only one tiny example, but I am sure that once a group begins to explore the text it will become clear that every single line is a goldmine of different ways of delivery, with countless possibilities of different emotional weights and colours.

With this style of theatre there are excellent possibilities for imaginative casting: there can certainly be cross-gender casting and there will be a different layer of meaning if, say, the giants are played by two males as opposed to two females or a male and a female. So, too, if Rainbow was black and the giants were white, this would add a particular slant. All such choices are open to the group and all have their validity. There is also the opportunity (in staging) for exciting and inventive use of group work — how do you depict crowds, heaps of bones, a cloud passing the moon or a huge gaping mouth using just bodies and voices?

It is a very physical form of theatre. But it can also be used as a reading exercise, free as it is from such things as stage directions, which often get in the way of a reading. Hopefully, in all the various forms that *Rainbow's Ending* may be used, it will provide a useful stimulus, through vocally and physically animated narrative, for discussion of its themes.

A Note on Casting

The speech paragraphs have been allocated to twenty participants in such a way as to give the group an even distribution of roles. I have allocated "character" parts throughout to particular letters (e.g. the two Giants are always speakers G and H, Rainbow is speaker T, etc). Please use the lettering only as a guideline: you may have a larger or smaller group than twenty, in which case you will need to re-allocate lines. There should be no problem with this if you keep in mind the basic rule (which can always be broken if you wish!) that the character always has those dialogue/narrative lines that relate to her or him. You may, though, find your own more interesting logic to line-distribution.

Scene Numbers

Scenes are numbered 1 to 25. This is not random: each new scene comes where, in my estimation, the story shifts on and perhaps a new mood needs to be created or a new dynamic created.

Noël Greig

Also by Noël Greig,
published by Samuel French Ltd:

Do We Ever See Grace?

RAINBOW'S ENDING

Scene 1

A There were two giants.

B They were huge.

C Enormous.

D Gi-normous.

E Gigantic.

F Anyway, they were very big.

G "I'm bigger than you," one of them boasted (and no kidding, this chap was as big as the Post Office tower).

H "Push off, titch," said the other (who was as high as the Empire State building).

G "Bet I can eat more than you at a go," boasted the first.

H "Oh yeah?"

G "Yeah."

H So they decided to have an eating competition, to see who could guzzle the most in one sitting.

G Mealtimes for giants lasted a couple of hundred years,

H So they shook hands,

G And agreed to come back when they'd had a good old tuck-in,

G
H } (*together*) And off they went.

I A little later in the day, a woman was sitting by the riverbank, with a fishing rod. It was a sunny day and the trout were almost queuing up to get themselves hooked.

G A couple of miles downriver, one giant lay down and started to lap up the water.

I "That's funny," said the fisherwoman, "the water's going down."

G "Slurp slurp," went the giant, as he drained the river dry, "come on little fishes, into my gob."

I So the fisherwoman packed up her tackle and trudged off to find another river.

H But there wasn't one, because the other giant had drained them all dry.

J Over the hill, a farmer was feeding his herd of cows

G When from out of the sky a mighty hand swooped down

K
L } (*together*) And up into the clouds went the cows.

G And, "Very beefy, very tasty," said the giant, as he marched off in search of the next course

J Leaving the farmer to mutter, "Ruddy giants, that's the second herd they've guzzled this week."

M And so it went on

N Week after week, month after month.

O "Where have all the buffalo gone?" the North American natives asked.

H But all they heard was a great big belch from behind the mountains.

P "What's happened to the whales?" said the deep-sea divers.

G And a great fat giant, lolloping on the seashore, smacking his greasy lips could have told them.

Q Nothing was safe from them.

R "They've started on the birds now," said someone.

S And everyone looked up at the empty sky and the silent trees.

T "I haven't seen a swan for years," sighed another.

H Meanwhile one of the giants had discovered the delights of melons, grapes and peaches, and was forcing several tons of each down his gullet. "Just a little snack," he burped.

G While the other was ripping up the banana trees and forcing them down his throat.

H (They were both getting pretty full by now and were staggering a bit.)

A By this time, people were getting fed up.

B "That's the trouble," someone pointed out, "we're not getting fed anything; it's these blasted giants who are getting fed up."

J "Look at the land," said the farmers, "it used to be fit to bust with fat cattle and ripe fruit. Now we're lucky to get half a dozen turnips from it."

P And those who made their living from the sea said, "We're happy if we catch two sprats and a sardine, these days."

K "Right, then," said another, "there's nothing for it. We'll have to go back to the cities."

L For a moment, nobody said a word.

M Then someone jumped up: "Oh, no, we won't," she declared.

K "We have to," said the first, "we've no choice. We could be safe there; big walls, that sort of thing."

M "The cities stink," said the woman.

N
O } (*together*) (Several people nodded in agreement.)
P

M And she continued, "Our ancestors left the cities to rot ages ago, and I don't blame them."

Q
R } (*together*) (More nods.)
S

M "We've all heard about cities, everyone crammed together, foul air, foul food, and besides …" She stopped.

Q Because everyone knew the stories, about how the cities had been abandoned

R After something dreadful had happened

S Something which was only talked about in whispers, at night.

T The general feeling was that they'd rather not go back to those places

A Until a chap who looked after the forests said, "They've started on the trees now."

K "There you are then," declared the one who had brought up the subject of cities, "that's put the lid on it. If there's no trees how can we build houses?"

B So, eventually

C After much discussion

D Nodding of heads

E Shaking of heads

F And general argy-bargy

I It was agreed: "The best thing for everyone is to go back and live in the cities, build strong walls and make do as best we can."

J And that was how, all over the world, from the plains of India to
the Downs of England, from the jungles of Africa to the coast of
Japan, the people packed up their pots and pans, turned their backs
on the wastelands which had once been their homes and trudged
off to the crumbling ruins amongst which their ancestors had once
lived.

SCENE 2

G The giants, on the other hand, were having their own problems.

H "The grub's running out," complained one.

G "It's not my fault," groaned the other (he was getting indigestion).
"If you will keep on stuffing yourself, then I'll not stop."

H (They could both hardly walk now, they'd crammed so much in.)

G "I'm not letting you win," said the other, shoving a plantation of
date-palms into his face.

H The first hadn't seen a date-palm in years and made a grab: "Give
me some of those."

G "Gerroff!"

H "Give 'em here."

G "Greedy pig."

H "Big lump of lard."

G If they'd not been so packed full of food

H All red in the face

G Lurching about

H They would have started walloping each other.

G As it was, they each gave a feeble swing

H And a half-hearted punch

G Then, with a wheeze

H And an "Uuurgh"

G They collapsed on the ground

H Like a couple of stranded whales. (Only there weren't any whales
any longer except the chewed up ones inside the giants.)

G And they fell asleep

H For a few hundred years

G Which was the giant equivalent of an after-dinner nap.

SCENE 3

K Meanwhile, the cities had come back to life.

L They grew and prospered, and one day, one of the leaders

M (Somehow there were people called leaders now)

L Said, "Since the countryside has been turned into a desert, we might as well see what use we can put it to."

N And a technical wizard said, "Here's my design for a type of machine which will dig up the ground so we can get at all the minerals beneath the surface. They will be useful to create even more machinery to produce little luxuries for us."

O Another clever spark pointed out that there were great mountains of bones littering the hills and valleys. "They are," he declared, "the remains of all the animals spat out by the giants. We can boil them down to produce a certain type of material, which can be turned into marvellous things."

P Everyone's eyes lit up at the thought of little luxuries and marvellous things.

Q "Bone-collecting working party, assemble!" yelled the works-master.

R And everyone assembled.

S "Neat straight lines!" bellowed the foreman.

T And everyone trudged off into the dusty plains to gather the bones of dead animals.

L "See," said a leader, "how safe we are behind our great high walls."

A (The walls were a bit too high to see the sun, unfortunately.)

L "And look," he continued, "how our lives are made beautiful and happy by the things we can make from the bones."

B And as time went on, some people could be heard singing the praises of the two great giants talked of in the stories.

ALL "Giants great and giants good, you left us bones to boil."

C It became the custom for a parent to take a small child to one side, and say, "There were once two giants …"

D And when the children covered their ears

C They laughed and said, "No, they were good to us, it was they who left seas of bones to harvest."

E So eventually the official religions of the cities were established, and the people prayed to the giants.

ALL "Dear giants, gentle giants
Send us today our bones to boil."

F Sometimes it happened that people from neighbouring cities disagreed about exactly what the giants were like.

I "They were very thin," said the thin people.

J "They were fat," said the fat people.

K "They had blue eyes," said the blue-eyed people.

L "They had curly hair," said the curly-haired people.

M Occasionally, these disagreements led to an intelligent discussion.

I Such as "Belt up!"

J "Or what?"

I "Smack in the gob."

J Oh yeah?"

I "Yeah!"

M And then there was a war.

SCENE 4

N One day, in one of the cities, in a dingy room in one of the darkest, dirtiest corners, lay an old, old woman. Older than anyone had ever known. She was dying.

O So old that some of the young people wouldn't go near her, saying, "She might die and make a mess all over my new shoes."

P Or, "She spoils the view."

Q Or, "She talks a load of rubbish."

N The old woman did talk a great deal, but hardly anyone could understand what she was talking of. She spoke of "the trees and the sweet water, full of fish, and the great white swans, which my own great-grandmother described to me, and the chalky cliffs where birds nested above the crashing waves and the spouting whales, and …"

R "Oh belt up, crow-features," whined her grandson, "you take up too much room in this flat and you smell of sweat and your breath stinks."

S But her granddaughter asked her more.

N And she talked about the giants.

S "I know about them," said the girl, "the gentle giants who left us bones to boil."

N "Vicious beasts, great cruel trampling things, great bloated things," replied the frail old woman, her eyes practically popping out of her head with anger.

S The granddaughter was shocked.

N "Great gorging monsters," went on the old woman, "damn them for ever and eternity, damn their eyes and their hearts and their stomachs. I'd like to see them split open with the sharpest knives and their bodies excavated."

R The grandson shot out of the door and shouted, "Help, the old girl's gone off her rocker."

N But she didn't hear, and cried out, "Split the damned things open from top to tail, let the whole world spill back out of their bellies."

T In ran a crowd. They'd heard how she'd blasphemed against the giants.

A "She'll poison the minds of the young," said the teachers.

B "She'll destroy the fabric of society," said the politicians.

C "She'll bring the revenge of the giants upon us," said the priests.

D "Kill her," said the lawyers.

E And they dragged her out into the main square

F Strung her up

I And strangled her

N And she was silent.

L "From now on," declared one of the greatest leaders, "once a year we shall sacrifice one of our number in this manner, so that the giants know we are loyal to them and thank them for their great gift of bones."

M And everyone said it was for the best.

S Except the granddaughter, who looked up at the dead body and said, "What's a swan, grandma?"

N But the corpse just turned in the breeze and said nothing.

SCENE 5

G In another part of the world, another breeze was blowing

H A foul-smelling breeze

G A stinking sort of breeze

H That sort of breeze that blows up when a couple of giants are snoring.

G "Snu-u-u-oorch, snu-u-u-oorch."
And are belching out great putrid blasts as they sleep

H "Bue-e-e-ughch, Bue-e-e-ughch."

G Flat on their backs they lay

H Smacking their lips in their sleep

G Slapping the flies which settled on their faces,
"Gerroff, nugh, ugh, gerroff!"

H "Wassat? Goway, ugh, ugh."

G The giants were beginning to stir.

H After several hundred years of after-dinner napping, they were starting to wake.

G Sit up

H Shake their heads

G Blink in the light.

H "That was a pretty fine tuck-in," yawned one.

G "Quite a slap-up," agreed the other, and stretched his arms.

H They were feeling peckish again.

G "Oh yer, I could sink my teeth into a few peacocks."

H "Or a couple of dozen baby elephants."

G "Or a school of dolphins."

H "Or a juicy pineapple plantation."

G And they decided to go in search of a few juicy tidbits, before they fainted with hunger.

H "Half a tick," said one, "there's something wrong."

G They stood and looked around them.

H "Where's all the green stuff gone?"

G "Where's all the plump beasties?"

H And they stood and gawped

G At the arid deserts where they had once seen mile upon mile of golden corn

H Wave upon wave of racing deer
G Flock upon flock of snow-white geese.
$\left.\begin{matrix}\mathbf{G}\\\mathbf{H}\end{matrix}\right\}$ *(together)* All gone.

H "Here, what about that?" said one, pointing to a huge mountain of bleached bones.

G "Oh yer," said the other, taking a closer look, "I remember that, it was a herd of hippopotami. I had to spit the bones out before I started on the cherry orchards."

H And they walked together across the continents and they saw nothing

G But dusty red wilderness

H Heaps of bones

G Great echoing ravines where rivers had once run.

H "This is an emergency," said one of them, "I'm famished, what'll we do?"

G The other was not listening. He was peering down at the ground and scratching his head. "That's funny," he muttered.

H "Naw, it's serious," said the other. "If we don't get some grub soon, we'll die."

G "I mean the trail of bones," said the first, and pointed to a little winding track across the scorched earth. "Look, there's bits of bones all dropped in a line along it."

H They peered into the dusty distance and saw that the track led on over the hills and the plains.

G So they followed it.

H Till one day they came to the top of a mountain and looked down.

G To where the track ended.

H "Looks like a garden wall," said one.

G "Let's see," said the other.

H And they approached the wall (which seemed quite an ordinary size to them, but which to us would seem to be knocking at the sky).

G And they peered over.

H "Look at them," whispered one, "it's those little things that look like us."

G And they looked down into the city.

SCENE 6

A Far below, in the dark and dirty streets, people were going about their business

B Making deals

C Making a noise

D Making love

E Borrowing money

F Lending money

I Rushing to work

J Rushing home

K Making love

L Getting arrested

M Sleeping in corners

N Quarrelling

O Shouting

P Crying

Q Laughing

R Dancing

S When someone looked up at the high, dark wall and pointed: "It's the giants," she cried.

T "Don't be daft," replied her neighbour.

S "I saw them," said the first, "I saw two great heads and four great eyes peeping out of the sky; it was them, they're coming back, just like it says in the Great Book," and she ran indoors and looked at the Book. "Look here," she said to her neighbour, pointing at the final chapter, "it tells how the giants will come back one day, to create a paradise for us to live in. I've seen them." And she rushed out into the main square and shouted, "I have seen the faces of the good giants. They have returned. We are saved."

A A great crowd gathered, to listen to her.

B And the rumour went round that something great was about to happen.

C "Let us pray," said the priests.

D So they knelt and prayed

C As the priest read from the Great Book which spoke of a new world emerging from the belly of the old, on the day when the giants returned.

SCENE 7

G Meanwhile, the giants had discovered that there were other cities, lots of them.

H "Busy little creatures, aren't they?" said one.

G "Oh yes, very industrious," said the other.

H And they travelled about for quite some time, peering over walls

G Laughing at the antics of the tiny creatures.

H "Something I can't understand," said one, "is why it is, whenever we pop our heads over and look at them, they start rushing about like they'd been stung?"

G "Odd, isn't it?" said the other. "Then they'll stop and kneel down with their eyes closed and their hands in front of their faces."

H "I wonder what that means?" said the first.

G "At any rate," remarked the other, "they're brave little chaps. If I was them and I saw a giant, I'd run and hide. I wouldn't kneel down in the open with my eyes shut."

H This seemed strange to both of them, so they spent a few moments of deep intellectual discussion on the matter.

G "Er ... Umm ..."

H "Yer, well ... Umm ..."

G "S'pose ... Yer ... Well ..."

H "Yer ... Mmm ... Er ..."

G This fascinating dialogue was interrupted, when two giant bellies began to rumble again.

H "Blerp, blerp."

G "Blech, blech."

H "Oh, beg your pardon."

G "No, please forgive me."

H They remembered how hungry they were.

G But what are they going to eat?

H A crafty look came into the eye of one, "I've got it."

G "What's that?"

H "Why those little chaps sit so still and don't run off."

G "Why's that?"

H "They're making us a gift."

G "What sort of gift?"

H "Sort of grub gift."

G "Grub gift, eh? What type of grub gift?"

H "Them."

G "Them?"

H "As grub for us. That's why they kneel and wait."

G "Wait for what?"

H "For us to grab 'em. Grub."

G "We've never grabbed them, ever."

H "Now's the time to start."

G "We can't."

H "Why not?"

G "They … They look like us."

H "Don't want to starve, do you?"

G "No."

H "Well then."

G "Not sure."

H "Hungry, aren't you?"

G "Yes."

H "Then it's us or them." And the first giant told what his grandfather had said: "Boy," he had said, "when it comes to the matter of survival, there's only one rule. And the rule is, Look After Number One."

G And they both agreed that this piece of wisdom made sense.

H So they came to a city and they peered over the wall.

G "See there," said one, "they're scuttling about. In a moment they'll stop and get down on their knees"

H "You're right," said the other, "look how still they are. Like they're all ready and waiting for us."

G So they reached down over the wall and into the heart of the city

H And plucked up a couple of handfuls of the little creatures.

G "See," said one, holding out his hand, "look at them all wriggling and writhing in my palm."

H "Plump little things, aren't they?" said the other.

G And, lifting their hands to their mouths, they opened wide their lips and stuck out their tongues, and tasted these new delicacies.

H "Mmmmm!" went one, chewing gently. "Nice and soft and tender."

G "Aaah!" sighed the other. "Lovely and juicy."

H And they sighed with satisfaction and swallowed them down.

G "A few more?"

H "After you."

G "No, no, after you."

H "How kind."

G "No need to fight over them, is there?"

H "No need at all, plenty of them."

G And down again went the great long arms, reaching into the streets and the houses.

T And that is how all the people of all the cities came to know that the return of the giants could be a terrible thing.

SCENE 8

C Whenever a city was visited by a giant, the priests would tell the people, "This is because some of you have sniggered at the Great Book and here is the punishment. It is your own doing."

D If news came that a giant was heading their way, the judges and magistrates ordered half a dozen people to be hung from the walls on butcher's hooks. "It's a sacrifice," they would say, "so the giant will see how we wish to serve it."

E If that didn't work, and the giant still made the city suffer, the leaders would declare: "It's because of the filthy behaviour of such-and-such a group living amongst us, it's their fault."

ALL "Kill them!" screamed the crowd.

F And the crowds would surge down the streets looking for the enemy within the walls, to kill them.

I If a city happened to be spared, and a neighbouring city was attacked, the lucky ones would say, "You see, they got what they deserved."

J And their leaders would say, "We always told you that lot in the next valley were an evil bunch."

K Or, "The fat people deserved the stuffing knocked out of them."

L Or, "That blue-eyed lot deserved to be wiped off the face of the earth."

M Or, "Those curly-haired degenerates got what was coming to them."

N Sometimes, in the dead of night, certain people could be seen slipping out of the cities. It would be some great leader or speaker, making their way across the rubble-strewn landscape, towards a sleeping giant. Then, standing on tiptoes, they would shout up to the giant's earhole something like, "When you get to our city, you'll find some quarters with red marks on their roofs. That's where you'll find the tastiest people."

G And the giant would smile down at the friendly little creature, saying, "Thank you for the tip. Put a green mark on your own roof and I'll make sure I don't grab any of your lot."

N And the leader would slip back through the city gates, sweating with relief.

O Next day an order would go out to the Chief of Police, "Put red marks on such-and-such a quarter."

P And the Chief of Police would grin, and say, "That bunch of perverts and trouble-makers? Sure." And he would amble off with his men to daub the roofs with red.

SCENE 9

G Over the years, the two giants made their separate ways across the continents of the earth.

Q Gradually, city after city fell silent

R As the last person was plucked, shrieking, from the streets, to be swallowed.

S Eventually, only two cities were left. They were hidden deep behind some mountains. They lay about a mile or so from each other.

H The giants had not found them

G Yet.

H One day, the giants saw each other. This was the first time they had met for fifty years or so.

G "How yer doin'?"

H "Not so bad."

G "Gettin' fed all right?"

H "Oh yer, couldn't be better."

G But they were both looking shifty.

H Neither of them had eaten for weeks. So when they said:

G "I've found an island chock-a-block full of the daintiest little villages."

H Or, "I've discovered half a continent crammed with little huts full of tasty tribes."

G They were both lying through their back teeth

H And they both knew the other knew it.

G So when they looked down and saw the two cities behind the mountains, the same thoughts occurred to both of them:

G }
H } *(together)* { "Right. That stinking pig's not going to have these." And, "Well then, if that heap of manure thinks he's getting his hands on them, he can think again."

G But they didn't say that. Instead they said:

H "Oh, look, here's a couple of fresh cities."

G "Oh, yes, so there are."

H "Peckish?"

G "Not really."

H "Me neither."

G All the same, they approached the cities, with greedy looks in their eyes.

H But making sure to smile sweetly at each other

G While in their hearts they were saying:

H "Rot his eyes, I'll finish him off."

G And, "I'll tear him limb from limb when I get the chance."

H Closer and closer they came

G Not taking their eyes off each other

H Until one pointed and said, "Look there, behind you, there's a whole load more cities."

G And the second turned round with a drooling look on his face.

H At which point, the first yanked up a small cliff and lobbed it at his friend

G Who yelled, "Ouch!", for the cliff had hit him behind the ear. "Right then, you asked for it!" he bellowed, picking up a rusty old bridge, and sending it crashing through the air

H To smash the other in the face.

G After which a reasonable discussion took place:

H "Clear off!"

G "Shan't!"

H "I saw them first!"

G "Naw you didn't!"

H "Yes I did!"

G "Prove it!"

H "All right!" The proof was a handful of boulders.

G The answer came in the form of a beachful of pebbles.

H "Aaargh!"

G "Ooooch!"

H "Uuuugh!"

G "Aaeeeiee!"

H And so, each crouched behind the outer walls of a city, the giants bombarded each other.

SCENE 10

T Meanwhile, as the rocks and boulders came crashing down on the cities, the people ran and hid in the deepest cellars.

A There in the damp and the dark, someone would sometimes hold up a candle. "These cellars," she would say, "are the oldest part of the city. They were here even before our ancestors returned to the city to rebuild it."

B And they told each other the stories of the time when the cities had laid deserted.

C And the time before that when the ancestors of their ancestors had built the cities.

D And the time when they, too, had crouched in cellars, hiding from something too terrible to even remember.

E "Just like us," whispered someone.

F And they shivered in the chilly place

I Waiting for the sound of destruction to stop.

G Occasionally, the two giants would get hungry. Then they would yell "Truce!" at each other

J And the cities would fall silent.

K But this was the worst time of all.

L "Don't speak," said mothers to their children.

M "Don't even breathe," whispered the older children to the young ones.

N And they listened, in the dark

G As greedy arms reached down over the city walls

H And greedy fingers scrabbled about in the ruins.

O Rustling sounds of something getting closer.

P People, wide-eyed with terror

Q Pressed against the walls.

G Fat fingers, poking about

R Getting nearer.

S People sweating with terror.

T A scream.

A Another scream.

B Howls of agony.

G As an enormous pink fist lifts up a handful or two

H Crams them into a mouth

G Chews and swallows.

H And then the battle would start again

G "Yeeow!"

H "Uuuaargh!"

SCENE 11

T We are sometimes told that before things can get better, they have to get worse.

A (Tell that to the natives of Brazil, whose ancient lands are destroyed by the giant roads.)

B (Tell that to victims of the plastic bullets in Ireland.)

C (Tell that to the dispossessed of the world, living in their refugee camps.)

D (Tell that to the hunted whales.)

E (Tell that to the forests which disappear daily.)

F Tell that to the people of the last two cities of the earth.

I One of the cities was named "Sycamore", after something called a tree, which used to exist, long before anyone could remember.

J The other was called "Dolphin", after some long-vanished creature.

K One night in Dolphin, as people sat in the dank basements, waiting for the great fat fingers to come scrabbling in the dark, someone said, "This is the end of us people."

L And someone else said, "Let's face facts, we're done for. Best to kill ourselves now."

M And people started to plan the least painful ways out of their lives.

T But in one gloomy corner sat a young woman, listening to all this talk. Rainbow was her name. "That's not right," she said to herself, "it doesn't make sense. Why should those great brutes make us give up our lives? Life should be sweet."

N Though when she spoke to others, they said:

O "You're being idealistic; there's nothing we can do about the situation."

P Or, "Wake up to reality and start thinking about slitting our own throat."

Q Or, "I'm going to strangle my babies tonight, after which I'll knock my brains out on the bricks."

T But she refused.

P And eventually a friend said, "I don't want to die, either, Rainbow."

Q And another agreed.

R And another

S Until a small band of them collected together and said, "Rainbow is right. Why should we die?"

P "But what can we do?" asked another. "They are so enormous, even our sharpest knives would be nothing more than a pinprick to them."

Q "We have no power, no strength," said another.

R And they looked at Rainbow

T Who shook her head. "There is something," she said, "but even the thought of it terrifies me. But if we have courage and cling together, it might succeed." And she leaned towards her friends.

S And they put their arms around each other in the gathering gloom

T And Rainbow whispered to them.

SCENE 12

A Outside of Dolphin, dusk settled on a bleak landscape of strewn rocks.

B Bones lay in deep drifts, bleached white.

C Heaps of human skulls lay thick.

G And in the midst of this ghostly litter lay a giant, sleeping, snoring, tired from the day's fighting and the evening's feasting.

O The moon rose and spread her light across the land. If you looked at her you might imagine that a small tear trickled down her face, as she gazed on the vision of hell spread out beneath her. "Poor earth," she could be saying, "where have all the great rustling forests gone, with their purple shadows? Or the rivers which I used to turn into liquid silver each night? Where are the nightingales? Where is the white barn owl which sat and watched in the velvet blackness?" And she mourned the tender dark of the night, full of the sounds of the creatures, full of mystery and beauty.

G The giant knew nothing of this. He opened his great greasy mouth and yawned in his sleep. A fat tongue lolled out and the stench of death rose from between his open lips.

O A cloud drifted across the moon, as if to veil her eyes from this obscenity.

P At that very moment, a small group of people were slipping out of a side-gate of the city.

T Rainbow and her friends

Q Picking their way across the rocks

R Carefully avoiding the fragile bones.

S "Oh Rainbow," whispered one, "these could be our friends, our families, our lovers."

T "Don't think of that," said Rainbow, "or we'll lose our courage. We'll have time to grieve and cry later, but right now we have something to do."

P And on they went

O And the moon came out to help them find what they were looking for.

Q "There it is," said one.

R And they stopped in their tracks and looked up

S And up

P And up

Q At a huge bulk, looming large, like a great cliff.

T The giant.

P "Rainbow, I'm scared," said one.

T "So am I," replied Rainbow, "so are we all. Let's admit it to each other, that's important. Then we can proceed without having to pretend."

Q And they all looked at each other

R And embraced each other

S For they knew that they might never see each other again

P For they were going into the jaws of death.

T "Now remember," whispered Rainbow, "what we agreed. If we cannot destroy it from the outside, then we must place ourselves within him and find a way to put an end to it. Look, see he's fast asleep and his mouth is wide open. That's our way in."

Q And they recoiled as a blast of putrid air rushed towards them.

T "The stink from his breath will guide us," said Rainbow.

R And they began to help each other up the mountain of heaving flesh

S Towards the mouth of the giant.

SCENE 13

O The sad moon sank beneath the mountains.

A A breeze stirred the rust-red dust of the plains.

B And in the east the first glimmers of light fingered into the sky.

C The sun rose.

D The heat hit the rocks like a hammer.

E In Dolphin, the people dragged themselves, pale and worn, from uneasy sleep.

F "Today we must end it," they said. "Today we must put an end to life, we cannot continue any longer."

I "Where's Rainbow?" asked one.

J "The fingers were close to her home, last night," came the reply. "She's probably gone."

K "Poor Rainbow," said the first, "she was a bit of a dreamer."

L And they agreed that Rainbow had never been a realistic person.
M So they went back to their preparation for suicide.

SCENE 14

P The people of Dolphin had not witnessed the events of the previous night, when
Q After an hour's climb, the friends at last reached the giant's mouth.
R And there they stood, on the lips
S Looking down into the ghastly cavern.
P A howling wind of filthy breath came rushing up, nearly knocking them off their feet.
Q So they clung together, shouting above the terrible noise, "Keep together, don't panic!"
T "Now then," called out Rainbow, "we must all hold on to each other and jump."
R And with one last look at the sky and the moon and the mountains, they held their breaths
S And jumped into the oozing pit.

SCENE 15

G The following morning, the giant yawned, stretched and gave a few snorts. "Uuuhmnnn," he went, "that was a nice little sleep." And he rubbed his eyes and began to look around for a rock, to start off the day's battle. "Funny," he said, and coughed a bit. Then he hemmed a bit and he hit his chest. "Must've got a bone stuck in my throat." Then he hawed a bit, and waggled his Adam's Apple. Then he swallowed a bit and said, "That's better," and with a "Yarroo!" he tossed a few boulders in the direction of the other city.

SCENE 16

P All of a sudden, Rainbow and her companions, who had been stuck in a very tight and smelly corridor, found themselves plunging down a wet and sticky tunnel.

Q They hurtled down and down, covered head to foot in a slimy substance.

R "Look," shouted one, "there's a sort of red light in the distance."

S "It's getting closer," yelled another.

T A cliff of wobbling white stuff reared up before them.

P "Wheee!" cried out the youngest, who was beginning to enjoy the ride.

Q They skidded down a slope of something green

P (The youngest thought it felt like jelly)

Q And fell headlong into a rushing red river.

R "It's blood," screamed one.

S "I'm drowning," called another.

Q "It's thick and sticky," howled a third.

T "Keep your heads up," replied Rainbow. "Swim hard."

P And swim they did, rushing on past dripping canyons of yellow and blue

Q Through great vaulted caverns of pink and orange

R Under throbbing roofs of pale silver.

P "I wonder," said the youngest, "if we're as colourful as this, inside."

T "Keep swimming," said Rainbow.

R At last the water became sluggish and they could breathe more easily.

S Then it ceased to move at all.

P They were in a huge, domed place, treading water in a great lake of crimson.

Q It was higher than any cathedral.

R From its arches and columns dripped slow gouts of red.

S Its walls were soft as red velvet cushions.

Q Its shadows were deep purple.

T "It's the heart," whispered Rainbow.

R And they looked around them in awe at the massive, silent place.

P "Look," said the youngest, "over there." And she pointed to a soft bank leading from the lake.

Q They waded through the liquid and on to the shore.

R And there in one corner of the place was a dark cave

S And within the cave, something they'd not seen before.

T They bent down and looked.

Q "It's a baby," said one.

P "It can't be," replied another. "Whoever heard of a baby inside a heart?"

S But they looked closer and it was a baby.

M A baby, so very delicate and small that its veins showed blue beneath its transparent skin, looking at them through great blue eyes.

T "Who are you?" asked Rainbow gently, stroking the tiny creature.

M "I am the giant's son," came the whispering little voice. "I have been here in his heart for as long as I could ever remember. It has been very lonely."

P "How did you come to be here?" asked the youngest one.

M And the creature told the story of its birth and its instant death.

SCENE 17

A A young mother lay with her newborn child in her arms.

B The father looked down and said, "He looks like a healthy kid, give him here and let's take a look."

A "Handle him gently," said the mother.

B "You bet," said the father and took the child. He looked down at it and thought to himself, "One day I'll have to die. One day I'll have to give up all the wonderful things of the world to this brat. Well, why should I?"

A "What's the matter?" asked the mother, who did not care for the crafty look in the man's eye.

B "Just thinking of when he's grown up and I'm an old dodderer, heading for the grave," he replied.

A "Kiss the child," said the mother.

B And the father chuckled and said, "Oh yes, I'll show him his daddy's fond of him."

A "I knew you'd love him," said the mother.

B "Oh, yes, I do, who wouldn't love a little shrimp that's going to make me count the days and months of the life I have left. Oh yes, I love him. I love him to death. I love him so much I could eat him."

A And opening his jaws, the father swallowed the son

B As the mother screamed, "No, no."

A But the man replied, "Now he will never never take my power away, and I will never never die."

B And with a blow he killed the woman, saying, "And I don't need you any longer, you hag. The world is mine. I'm here for ever."

SCENE 18

M "And that," said the child, "is how I lost my mother and lost my life. I exist inside this place and will never know what the world is like."

P The friends were very silent.

T Rainbow spoke: "We're going to kill your father. We're going to rip him open. Look here . . ."

Q And they showed the baby the knives they had with them.

M "Good," said the child.

S "We'll take you with us," said one. "You can come and live in the world with us."

M But the creature refused, saying, "I'd like that, but there is something you must know. I have a heart too, and all it has had to do, over these thousands of years, is to dwell on the hate I have for my father. That is all I have ever known. I'll bring that with me into the world, and I know I could never learn to love. It's too late, I'm poisoned with it. Believe me, eventually I'd turn on you and destroy you." And he turned his face away and cried and wouldn't speak any more.

T So Rainbow led her friends away, and they continued their journey.

SCENE 19

C Over Dolphin City the sky was grey. A thick blanket of sullen clouds lay packed like army blankets from horizon to horizon.

D The people pulled their rags about them, as they trudged to the main square

E Where the head leader was perched on a high platform. "People of Dolphin," he said, "your leaders have been discussing the situation."

F And the other half-dozen wizened heads on the platform nodded.

E "For some time," he continued, "there has been talk of mass suicide. But we are opposed to this."

I "Oh ay," snorted someone, "you've not suggested anything else."

K "Oh, yes, they have," chimed in a third, "they've suggested we get in lines and march to work."

L And a fourth added, "And they've suggested to their police and their soldiers who should get arrested and shot."

D "Ssh!" whispered a fifth, "that's the leaders, show a bit of respect."

E "Well now," spoke out the leader, "here's something we do suggest. From now on, anyone found committing suicide will be committing treason, and will be instantly executed."

K A woman in the crowd shouted out, "What's that supposed to mean, it's baby talk!" and she held her small child up.

L And the baby went, "Goo-goo, ga-ga, glurg-glurg."

K "See!" said the woman. "She's an intellectual compared to that lot up on the platform!"

E "Arrest her!" screeched the leader.

F And a soldier dragged her away.

E "That," continued the Great Man, "is what can be expected by anyone else who interrupts."

C On to the platform stepped the Great Priest of Dolphin, his green eyes shining like beacons. "People," he boomed out, "there is a meaning behind this mighty battle that is raging."

B "Sure," muttered someone, "it means we're all being pummelled into the dust."

C "And the meaning is," went on the Great Priest, "that when we prayed to the Good Giants, we were mistaken."

B "You don't say?" said the mutterer.

C "But the fact is," boomed out the Priest, "there is a Good Giant and a Bad Giant. The Good Giant is fighting on behalf of the Good People, the Bad Giant fights on behalf of the Bad People."

A } (*together*) Several babies went, "Goo-goo, ga-ga, glurg-glurg."
B }

E "Arrest those babies!" howled the leader.

F And soldiers tore the babies from their mothers' arms

I And threw them against the walls.

C The Priest continued, "Forget your despair. We are offering salvation. Our Giant fights on our behalf, he needs our help."

E "And so," cried out the leader, "our great task is to cross the plains to Sycamore and enter that city, armed with weapons, to set every man, woman and child in that place to death. We must join forces at once with our Giant, to end this terrible conflict, to save the world."

B "Not me," muttered the mutterer, "I'm not doing any giant's dirty work for him."

A "Sorry, mate," said a soldier, "we've orders to shoot anyone who doesn't obey."

K And the people were marched out of the city.

L "Tell me this," whispered someone to her neighbour, "didn't they say there was a Good Giant and a Bad Giant?"

J The other nodded, "Yes."

L "But they didn't say which was which, did they?

J "No."

L "So what d'you reckon?"

J Dunno. S'pose they meant ours was the good one. No point fighting for the bad one, is there?

L "But they didn't say, did they?"

J "No, but …"

L "No talking in the ranks," yelled a soldier.

M And they all looked across the plains to Sycamore.

E "Citizens," cried out the leader (safe behind the city walls), "by tonight you will have performed a great service to humanity."

F "Charge!" yelled the General.

E "Let's get back to the basements," said the leaders.

A And the citizens of Dolphin, weary and dirty, staggered across the plains towards Sycamore.

SCENE 20

T Rainbow and her friends knew none of this.

P For some time they had been moving along a high, curved tunnel

Q Feeling their way along the walls

R Till they reached a point where several smaller tunnels led off in different directions.

S "This way …"

P "No, that way …"

Q "What about down there?"

R They were lost.

P "What are we going to do?" whined the youngest. "We should have stayed at home."

Q Then they heard a sound. Something unlike any other they had ever heard.

R Look!" said one, pointing up.

A High above them was something blue and darting.

T "So beautiful," whispered Rainbow.

P But they did not know what it was.

A For bluebirds had vanished from the earth and vanished from memory, many centuries ago.

T "Here, little creature," said Rainbow, holding out her hand.

R "It could be dangerous," said one, cowering. "Be careful."

T Somehow Rainbow didn't think so. In a moment it was nestling in her palm, its tiny breast beating. She stroked it, and it flew into the air again, singing. "It's leading us," she said.

A And it flew ahead of them, down a tunnel.

P So they followed it

Q Closer and closer to the end of the tunnel

R Nearer and nearer to the edge of the space beyond.

S And there they were

T Looking out across a mighty cavern

P And what they saw they did not recognize

Q Although perhaps they did, for they smiled and then looked puzzled.

R "That's odd …"

S "I'm sure I …"

T It's like something I dreamt of, once …"

P For what they were looking at within the vast belly of the beast

Q Was the world

R The world that had been lost.

S And they gazed upon great rivers of dancing fish

T Wild green plains with grazing cattle

P Herds of gazelles

Q Flocks of geese

R Wave upon wave of lemon groves

S Winding vines heavy with fat grapes

T Carpets of roses

P Canopies of oak

Q And there were no words to describe the beauty of it.

R So they stood and looked

P And the youngest brushed aside a tear, saying, "I want to bring my mother here, she'd like it."

T "Better still," said Rainbow, "we'll take it to your mother." And she took out the sharp blade hidden in her boot

Q And the others took out their knives

A And they looked up, and the bluebird was singing and leading them on again.

SCENE 21

B It was noon, and the parched earth between Dolphin and Sycamore threw dust into the air.

C The people gasped for air: "We need water."

D "Get on," shouted a soldier and lashed out with a whip.

E Overhead the rocks crashed through the air

F And in the distance a cloud of red dust approached.

I "It's the people from Sycamore," panted someone, "they're coming to kill us."

J "They're doing the same," screamed another, "they're coming to kill us."

K And the two tattered armies approached each other

L Lashed by whips

M Beaten across the heads by guns

G When suddenly a terrifying howl split the air.

L Then silence.

G Then another howl of pain.

M Everyone looked back to Dolphin

G To see, towering above it, the giant, clutching at his side, staggering, first this way, then that.

M No-one moved

G As the mountain of flesh stood swaying, a terrible look on his face, groaning and moaning, his lips pulled back, his teeth clenched.

E Inside the city the leaders and the priests shouted up at the giant, "Keep fighting, we're on your side, look at the citizens marching towards the enemy. Don't weaken, we're going to win."

G But the giant heard nothing. Still as stone he stood, beads of sweat falling from him, his eyes staring.

SCENE 22

T No wonder. For within the folds of his flesh sharp instruments were at work

P Hacking at the walls of fat

Q Cutting through blubber

R Digging into sinews

S Excavating the heaving mass

T Ripping through purple veins

S Deeper and deeper.

T "Keep going."

P "Don't give up."

Q "Rip right through."

R "Nearly there."

S Faster and faster they went, as if the devil were at their heels.

B Nothing moved, except the fine red dust settling on the terrified masses

G Looking up at the beast in his agony, grabbing at his belly, wiping the sweat from his eyes, crying out in a terrible roar, "He-e-e-elp!"

SCENE 23

T From within, Rainbow and company heard a faint echo:

G "He-e-e-elp!"

T "No help for him now," said Rainbow, pointing. "Look, there's yellow and gold shining through the wall; it's the sun. One more effort and we're there."

R And with a final lunge the last layer tore apart

S And they covered their ears, as the sound of flesh ripping open filled the air.

SCENE 24

G Slowly the giant stared down at his own belly. A long tear shot across it, and the walls flew apart.

J And the people stared in amazement as they watched the contents spill from the sky and down to the waiting earth.

K For what seemed like an age they watched as the whole of creation spilled from the gaping wound

L Turning the land to green

M The gullies to gushing rivers

N The canyons to lush valleys

O The silent hills to banks of colour

J The wastelands to waving plains of corn and barley

K The empty skies to a net of flying creatures

L The deserts to waving forests.

G And when it had finished, the giant turned gently on his heels, stared a moment, brushed his hand across his face.

E "Don't weaken," howled the leaders, from the highest towers of Dolphin.

G But he did not hear. He simply sighed, and closed his eyes. Then he tottered slightly.

E "Don't fall this way," screeched the leaders.

G The giant fumbled around near his belly, sighed again, lifted his hand to his mouth, then staggered again.

E "Mercy!" shrieked the leaders.

G But down he came, crashing through the sky towards the city, shattering its buildings to their foundation.

K And then again, silence.

SCENE 25

B Slowly the crowds struggled to their feet. People from the two cities gathered together, helping each other.

C They rubbed their eyes and looked around them at the miracle of colour.

D Then, as one, they turned to Sycamore

H Where, crouched behind its walls, was the other giant. A greedy look spread across his face as he surveyed the rich lands stretching out across the world.

F "What'll we do?" people moaned. "He'll destroy it all."

K "No?" cried out a voice. "Look here!" and he held out a bloody dagger, explaining how they came to kill the beast, describing the journey.

J Then a shadow blotted out the sun. They turned once again

H As the living monster began to slowly rise up, eyes glinting, lips smacking.

B "Where's Rainbow?" someone cried. "She'll have the answer."

C Rainbow could not be found.

A Just then, a bluebird flew past, turned, came back, then flew on again.

B They followed it

C To the broken corpse of the giant, stretched out across the ruined city

D To the fist, lying close to the gaping mouth

E To the sight of a small, crushed body within that fist.

T To Rainbow.

R "His hand came down, just as we were getting out," said one of the friends.

P "Rainbow," whispered the youngest, "can you hear us? Are you dead?"

T Rainbow's eyelids fluttered slightly.

S "Rainbow," they whispered, "we succeeded."

T Rainbow smiled gently.

Q "But Rainbow," they continued, "there's the other monster on the horizon. What'll we do this time? We've got half of the world back, we don't want to lose it. Tell us."

T Rainbow opened her lips and whispered, "I …"

P "Yes?"

T "I … I … was having a dream. I dreamt I killed a giant."

P "You did. Now there's another. How can we get rid of it?"

T "That's your dream," whispered Rainbow, "I don't know how it ends." And she lay back her head, closed her eyes and fell asleep forever.

F A soft rain began to fall. The evening sun turned the sky to roses.

A A bluebird flew up into the sky.

B They turned and looked.

H A great purple shape loomed above Sycamore, its bloodshot eyes glinting, a low chuckle emerging from its throat.

K The people looked towards it.

M Behind the creature, in the distant sky, at the edge of the rain and the sun, a band of bright colour appeared.

A A rainbow. And a small bird singing beneath its arch. As if saying, "This way, this way."

N And the great crowds stood together and moved towards the great shambling brute in their path

O Moved off as one person towards the giant.

K Facing the monster

L Or following the rainbow?

A Who knows?

THE END